QUICK TIPS

— FOR —

BUSINESS GROWTH

100 QUICK TIPS

FOR

BUSINESS GROWTH

JOHN W. MYRNA

This book is dedicated to the hundreds of organizations and thousands of executives who have inspired these insights.

Tip #1: The CEO has only 3 permanent jobs:

1) Develop the executive team.
2) Make the "you bet the company" decisions.
3) Lead the strategic planning process.

After those jobs, CEOs contribute where the company doesn't yet have (or can't afford) resources, or where they have special competence or interest.

Tip #2: CEOs are generally intuitive and smart. They know exactly what needs to be done after hearing only a bit of the problem. They are also prone to action and hence don't want to waste time waiting for the rest of the team to catch up. The effect is that others see themselves executing a plan they don't understand.

Bite your lip, have patience, and hang in there until the rest of the team catches up with you. They will do a better job, and, who knows, maybe your intuition wasn't right after all.

Tip #3: Be warned that for many people, questions about their work implies mistrust.

Be sensitive to this perception. Good people have quit when they became convinced they weren't trusted merely because they were always asked where the numbers came from and how they reached their conclusions.
Be sensitive to that perception and be prepared to explain your motivations whether you are just curious about how things work, or you are validating their conclusions.

Tip #4: When you extend your product market strategy make sure you understand today's reality. Are you in a new market or do you merely have a large customer? Do you have a new product or merely a custom solution? You are not in a new market until you have multiple customers there.

Tip #5: The 80/20 rule, also called Pareto's Law, is derived from theories and empirical studies of Italian economist and sociologist Vilfredo Pareto (1848-1923).

If you want to excel, you must understand the 80/20 Rule and how to apply it to your business:

THE RULE: 20% of any "population" produces 80% of the results.

- 20% of your actions, investments or efforts produce 80% of your results.
- 20% of your sales force produces 80% of your sales.
- 20% of your customers cause 80% of your late collections.
- 20% of your suppliers cause 80% of late deliveries.
- 20% of your customers produce 80% of your sales and profits.
- 20% of workers cause 80% of complaints.
- 20% of your customers register 80% of complaints . . . etc.

Tip #6: There is a quick strategy for taking hold of an organization.

Focus your sales VP on contacting the top 20% of your company's customers every month. If the list is too large, focus on the top 20% of the top 20%. Do the same for accounts payable and inventory.

Only 20% of your business is the current core producing 80% of your good and bad results. You should be able to easily manage one-fifth of the current organization.

Tip #7: Support goals that reach beyond today, this year, this decade, and even your life. The bigger the dream the longer it may take to accomplish, but if you keep making a little progress every year the goal will ultimately be achieved.

Tip #8: Running a business by looking only at the past ("Don't fix what isn't broken, it's always worked before, stay with what you know, don't change horses in midstream," etc.) is like steering a ship by looking only at the wake.

It's very easy to steer a straight course that way, but sooner or later you'll collide with something and sink your ship/business.

Whatever's out front is changing. You better be ready to change too.

Tip #9: The future leaves muddy footprints in the present. Read the "developments to watch" section in trade publications. Most overnight sensations have been in development and discussed for years.

Ask yourself what high-growth product will become economically feasible in five years that you can become a leading supplier if you initiate development now.

Tip #10: Manage and account for development separate from operations. Operate the business with margins healthy for your business. It's ideal when you can develop new markets and products using the current profits of your core business.

But be careful.

Don't assume that weak profits are due to investment. It is just as likely that you are subsidizing inefficient operations with disastrous long-term effects.

Tip #11: Take care in administering resources at the senior level. There are not enough titles, time, compensation, power, equity, and security to distribute equally.

Care and creativity must be applied in matching those limited resources with the needs, motivations, and contributions of your senior people.

©Myrna Associates Inc.

Tip #12: Every organization has two constant challenges: **communication** and **focus**. Those aren't problems to be solved, but ongoing challenges to attend to.

Tip #13: When a problem exists mainly because of poor communication, try to solve it immediately by bringing all the parties together. Call the group into your office for a short meeting. If some are in out-of-town offices, get them on the speaker phone or Zoom for a conference call. Serve as a facilitator to get issues aired and a solution decided quickly.

Tip #14: Save everyone's anxiety worrying about where they stand in your regard. *Always* use alphabetical distribution lists on memos, letters, reports, etc.

Tip #15: Share your goals. Employees can help you reach your goals only if they know what those goals are.

Tip #16: There is no silver bullet that will solve your communication challenge.

You must create and use every possible communication approach:

- quarterly company meetings
- annual company picnic
- annual holiday party
- annual performance reviews
- monthly reporting internal newsletter
- weekly one-on-one meetings with reports
- regular executive meetings
- temporary task forces
- walking around communal areas

Tip #17: Serve high-fat, high-calorie foods like donuts when you want a group to slow down and tune out. Serve low-fat, low-calorie foods like bagels when you want to keep a group sharp.

©Myrna Associates Inc.

Tip #18: Flow time is a state you enter when you are concentrating well and working without distracting thoughts or outside disturbance. You flow along with getting things done. It takes about 20 minutes to achieve the "state" of flow time. One interruption drops you out and restarts the 20-minute clock. That's why it's so hard to complete anything that requires sustained concentration at the office.

Tip #19: How to Protect Flow Time:
1) Discuss the concept of flow time with your coworkers and solicit their support.
2) Turn off your telephone, computer e-mail and other electronic sources of interruption.
3) Place a "Do not disturb, I'm in flow time" notice on your closed door with a time when you will be available again.

If you were out to lunch no one would interrupt you; can't you simulate that state while you work on a project that requires flow time?

Tip #20: Keep It Simple Stupid (KISS)! A good rule of thumb is that only the projects that appear easy to do are in fact possible.

Tip #21: When estimating, remember these rules of thumb:

1) Everyone thinks they can complete 10 times as much as they actually have time to do. Only 1 item on your to-do list of 10 will get finished.
2) If you estimate a project in months, you will underestimate it by a factor of 2.6.
3) If you estimate a project in days, you will estimate it by a factor of 1.3.
4) If you estimate a project in hours, you will Overestimate it because you round up each odd hour.

Tip #22: Quality and satisfaction exist only in reference to customer expectations.

A service rating of 7 can represent quality if customers expect only a 5. A service rating of 7, on the other hand, is unacceptable if customers expect a 9!

To improve quality, you can increase performance and/or lower expectations. In too many cases, customer expectations are allowed to run unchecked to a point that no level of performance is perceived as acceptable.

Tip #23: In general, hire slowly and fire fast. Take the time to identify the best person for the job. Act fast if it becomes clear that someone isn't working out.

Tip #24: Watch your head count.
Peter Drucker estimated an employee generates a total of 3 times his salary in expenses. (Employees need desks, paper, phones, water, benefits, management, etc.) An employee with an annual salary of $33,333 adds $100,000 in bottom-line expenses. An annual mistake of just one too many employees can be what's keeping your company from being profitable.

Tip #25: Remember that continuous improvement applies to your people as well as your processes. You should have a strategy to increase employee productivity every year. Coaching, training, and utilization of new tools like AI can enable you to double the business without doubling the workforce.

Tip #26: Beware of unknown unknowns. Strategic planning is a major aid in identifying issues your executives didn't know that they didn't know existed.

Tip #27: Life is unfair. You can't design and build a perfect product until after it is built and in the hands of customers. Only with feedback from real users do you have enough information to properly design a new product. So? Get the first version done quickly and into the hands of users. Listen carefully, then respond quickly with minor or major changes.

Tip #28: The design of a new product starts when you are "finished", and the first real customer puts it to work. Plan for that. Don't reassign your development team when the first version is released; that is exactly when you need them free to focus on initial customer reaction.

Tip #29: Goals are accomplished because of a champion. Never undertake a major project unless you have a champion committed to shepherding the project to completion. Remember, people can be the champion of only one goal at a time; you are fooling yourself to think otherwise.

Tip #30: Focus on the important, not just the urgent. One way to accomplish important tasks is to create a natural deadline that makes them urgent as well as important.

Tip #31: The easiest way to predict the future is to create it. Take control and become proactive. Don't manage by watching the wake and projecting the future; stand on the bow of your boat, pick a star to steer by, and go for it. Ad astra per aspera (to the stars through difficulties).

Tip #32: People desperately want to know if you understand and consider their thoughts and opinions before you make a decision. They rarely insist you follow their suggestions. Actively solicit the opinions of those affected by a decision *before* you make the decision. It builds trust and usually leads to a better decision.

Tip #33: There is an old wife's tale that if you drop a frog into a pot of boiling water, it will leap out. If you put that frog in a pot of warm water and slowly increase the temperature, the frog will cook. That is the reason a new CEO, employee, consultant, or even visitor can spot a company's problem and/or better way of doing an operation. Experienced "old-timers" can be like that frog. They can be on the verge of bankruptcy yet never notice it. Periodically step away for a long view, bring in outsiders unlikely to agree just to be nice, and join CEO network groups like the CEO Club, Presidential Advisory Councils (PAC), or Vistage to get that fresh frog's opinion.

Tip #34: Don't spend dollars chasing pennies. Remember that the relevant dollar figure changes as you grow. Ford's accountants don't worry about discrepancies less than a million dollars. Are you still investing your company's energies micromanaging $5, $10, and $20 expenditures?

Tip #35: For productive recurring management meetings, follow these four rules:

1) Start meetings by setting the agenda. Take 5 minutes or less for this. Rank items and follow the agenda in order.

2) End meetings on time, even if they start late. Agree that a meeting scheduled for Mondays, 8 to 9 am always ends at 9 am no matter where you are on the agenda or how late you start.

3) End discussion when it drifts to a topic concerning less than all the attendees.

4) Distribute "action items only" minutes immediately after the meeting. (Timeliness is more important than precise grammar or even spelling.)

Tip #36: Always use a facilitator for important, multi-day meetings.

1) You can't afford to waste your time.
2) You can't afford to waste your team's time.
3) You can't afford the opportunity costs of not achieving the planned results.

A true facilitator is like an arbitrator, neutral in having no vested interest but also the plus of an expert in the details of meeting management.

Tip #37: How many strategic goals can a company handle? Not more than 5 to 10 and never more than the number of members of the executive team. Strategic goals can only be championed by members of the executive team.

Tip #38: Balance market and technical risk. Sometimes the marketing risks of not hurrying a product to the market far exceed the technical risks of fielding a "not quite ready for primetime" offering. Such a time may be when a company is in a do-or-die cash crunch, or the market window is short, and the competition is close on your heels. At other times, the risk of shipping a product with major flaws can be the death of a company. Such a case might be products that affect personal or asset safety. In any case, assess and accept risk carefully and plan to react quickly as you receive market feedback.

Tip #39: Declare the "crisis" over. Every business has a predictable number of "unpredictable" crises. Deliveries get lost, computers crash, customers don't read the manual and payments are late. What appears at first to be a "crisis" may, in fact, just be part of the way it is.

Tip #40: Avoid custom software. In most cases, it's better to adjust your business practices slightly to exploit a commercial package than it is to pay to program a custom solution. This year's leading-edge, expensive custom application can become next year's albatross, holding you back from keeping up with your competitors. People cherish obsolete hardware or software when they pay a lot for it.

Tip #41: People do not naturally connect the dots. As often as not, they attribute success to luck or some other random event. When reporting or celebrating a success always tie that success back to specific strategies, actions, or behaviors. That builds trust and belief in your plans and planning, enhancing their implementation.

Tip #42: If your company can't be first in its market, define and develop a new market definition where you can be first! Find a niche in your current market where you can be first, and tailor your product to fit the niche.

Tip #43: Improving things, a little at a time for most projects, is usually a far better approach than waiting for the perfect solution. W. Edwards Deming seldom used the term "Quality Control." His favorite term was always "Continuous Process Improvement." Don't think of a process as a problem to be solved. A process is something to constantly improve. Quality has no finish line.

Tip #44: Don't over-specify a project. Over-specification makes you a supervisor, as your employee attempts to duplicate how you'd do the project. Instead, pride yourself on details you allow to be treated in a creative way. Sure, the final result will be different than if you had done it yourself, but seldom worse. In fact, you may discover that the employee is better than you — a real productivity gain.

©Myrna Associates Inc.

Tip #45: Share your numbers. Your employees have guesses and those guesses are usually more optimistic than reality. Sometimes for fun ask a dozen people what a typical supermarket's profit margin is. Just about everyone guesses higher than the real value of less than 3%.

Tip #46: Expect executives to have one motto: No surprises. Make sure your execs keep you informed. Learn to take in *all* news like hearing a weather report. You want to know if it's raining so you can take an umbrella. If you bite someone's head off for telling you about a storm you will surely get "wet."

Tip #47: Strategic planning is **not** about brainstorming. Strategic planning is **not** about innovation. Strategic planning **is** about focusing on the day-to-day, month-to-month, and year-to-year running of the business in order to achieve long-term goals. It should be routine.

Tip #48: Too many companies force employees to jump through special hoops when making a capital purchase of $10,000, $25,000, or $50,000, while never thinking twice about letting them hire a $33,333 per year new employee that costs the company's bottom line $100,000 per year. Pick a financial level requiring formal control and be consistent across *all* forms of financial commitment. Make *sure* everyone knows the few decisions you reserve for yourself. Most CEOs reserve only these 3:

1) Making the final hiring decision.
2) Binding the company to a major financial commitment.
3) Making "you bet the company" decisions.

Tip #49: Don't waste time assigning blame. It makes your company team defensive and wastes time. Focus instead on understanding the current problem and where we go from here.

Tip #50: If you fill a coffee cup to the brim, you will either spill coffee on the way back to the office or take an inordinate amount of time tiptoeing down the hall. Capacity is reached at 80%, not 100%. When you schedule any resource beyond 80%, instead of gaining you will lose more from juggling, restarting, and rescheduling.

Tip #51: Consider your sales history a corporate asset. Prospect names, contact history, previous sales, etc. should be recorded on a computer database. This way you don't lose momentum when a salesperson gets sick or leaves. Also, you can institute automated processes to constantly reach prospects who "raised their hand" in the past. The only way to motivate your sales team to keep records is to have a system that makes it *in their best interest* to maintain the data. Design the system to first meet the sales team's needs. Management's use will follow.

Tip #52: There is *power* in practicing *Acts of Random Recognition*. Keep a stack of thank-you cards and $50/$100-dollar bills in your desk. When you discover someone doing something special, jot down a few words and put the card with cash in their in-box. Everyone loves to be recognized. Often the thank you card with its recognition of a specific action will be saved, savored, and posted.

Tip #53: Employee behaviors that are rewarded and activities that receive your attention speak strongest. By all means, give speeches and write memos but remember that people respond to what your actions are rather than what you say.

Tip #54: Regularity beats quantity every time. It is far better to do a 2-page newsletter every quarter than to publish an 8-page work of art once, and then lack the resources to follow up with another issue.

Tip #55: Always demand dates for results. Dates are a commitment, a form of communication, and a reality check. But, *never, never* use dates as a club.

Tip #56: Things happen because of deadlines. A deadline that is tied to an external event like April 15 is a more powerful mover than an arbitrary "scientifically derived" deadline produced by a PERT chart or other project-management technique. To get important tasks done, create a natural deadline that makes the task both urgent and important.

Tip #57: Everything happens because of a champion. Undertake a major project only if you have a champion committed to shepherding the project to completion. Remember, people can be the champion of only one goal at a time.

Tip #58: What does the DATE communicate in an action plan?

A date is accountability.
A date is assessment.
A date is commitment.
A date is communication.
A date is efficacy.
A date is expectations.
A date is external imposition.
A date is momentum.
A date is negotiation.
A date is reality.
A date is results.
A date is success.
A date is a tool.
A date is urgency.
A date is value, based on time.

Tip #59: When planning, use clear milestones. A milestone is either reached or not. There is *one* person responsible for a milestone even though many may be working on it. A milestone *always* carries a completion date.

Tip #60: A plan is a reality check. You can be sure that the future won't exactly play out the way you wrote the plan, *but* how can you have confidence in your goal if you can't create a plausible, defensible scenario of how you could reach it?

Tip #61: The profit margin in a developing business is worse than in a mature business. Be careful not to fall into the MBA's trap of "optimizing" products based on their current profitability.

That's eating your seed corn.

Tip #62: A strategic plan is like a pilot's flight plan. The flight plan identifies the ultimate destination and major milestones along the way. As with a flight plan, you must know that your location at any given moment won't be exactly on the plan; you will be ahead, behind, East or West of the route. *But* you still know where you're going and you will, with the plan, know when your drift from the route becomes extreme.

Tip #63: If you have a problem employee, close your eyes, and imagine what life would be like without them around. If the negatives outweigh the positives, move them to a job in a different location or in another company.

Tip #64: An executive is someone who looks at the business through the eyes of the CEO.

Tip #65: Remind yourself of the current costs of success. For startups, there is a steep learning curve with the obligation of working long hours. For growth, there is the "cost" of working through others. Are you ready to pay those prices? If you can't accept those costs, change the situation. Get big or stay small, but don't whine about the "costs."

Tip #66: To thine own self be true. In other words, don't waste time trying to correct your personal weaknesses. A golfer dropped 10 points from his game when he stopped trying to drive "correctly" and instead played his slice. It is easier to adjust for your known bias than to change it.

Tip #67: The only way to have a true competitive advantage is to be the lowest-cost producer of the best product. Learn (research) to produce the best product in your market and sell more of them than anyone else. Learn (practice) to make that product at lower cost than any of your competitors.

Tip #68: Force yourself to offer a 100% money-back guarantee. It is the most powerful statement of quality in existence.

Tip #69: Don't ask for reports and measures unless you know exactly how you will use the data. There's a cost to gathering and reporting data, and so-called "historical" data is seldom useful when you finally get around to reviewing it.

Tip #70: The answer "It's impossible" usually means "I don't know how to do it" or you're asking the wrong question. The world is full of once-impossible things that are commonplace today. So-called laws of physics once prevented man from flying, from escaping earth's gravity, or transmitting data over a telephone line at more than 1,200 bits per second, yet *today* we have rovers on Mars, the sky full of airplanes, and data can be transmitted at 56,000 bits per second over a phone line.

Tip #71: The value of groups is in the discussions, *not* the voting. As the old story goes, six blind men tried to understand what an elephant was. Each in turn thought the beast was a wall, a spear, a fan, a tree trunk, a snake, and a rope. All were right and yet all were wrong. It takes everyone involved to create a true picture of an elephant. It takes everyone involved to create a true picture of an issue.

Tip #72: Make things look as important as you consider them. A critical company plan that is distributed as a stack of poorly photocopied and stapled sheets will mask the plan's importance. A laser-printed master with a clean font, a simple cover, double-sided pages, and GBC bound will *dramatically* improve your message.

Tip #73: Ask a person's opinion only if you're prepared to consider it.

Tip #74: Present only key points in formal presentations—20% of your points are 80% of the value. Let the audience question you on their choice of specific points. As the audience hears your answers to their specific questions, they will grow to trust the premise of your entire presentation. 50% of your presentation pushing the key 20% of points and 50% responding to specific questions from the audience.

Tip #75: A budget is a financial model of how a company might achieve its annual financial goals. It demonstrates that there is a believable balance between planned revenue and required resources. A normal budget is based on running a financial model with one set of assumptions. A flexible budget retains the model's logic and calculates monthly budgets by rerunning it with actual values for year-to-date measures. Flexible budgeting simplifies maintaining control even if sales are significantly higher or lower than anticipated.

Tip #76: Profit is the value we create from our use (stewardship) of resources consumed. **Value** equals **Revenue** minus **Expenses**. If the long-term **Value** we create is *negative*, the market is telling us we have no justification for existence. If a product isn't creating value, give those resources to something that can.

Tip #77: Remind senior executives that they assume greater responsibilities and risks along with greater titles and compensation.

Tip #78: Don't call in during your vacation. This is an excellent time to find out what breaks when you aren't looking. Fix it when you return. By all means, leave an emergency number, but only for a true emergency.

Tip #79: Turnover isn't necessarily bad. There are good reasons for employees to leave. It's acceptable to leave for opportunities the company can't provide or for exceptional pay. It's OK to leave because the employee and the company have grown in different directions or at a different pace. Finally, it's OK to ask a new employee to leave if it's clear in the first 90 days that despite both parties' best efforts, the fit and chemistry just aren't right. It's not acceptable that someone leaves because you did a sloppy hiring job, to obtain something that your company could have granted or because of abusiveness.

Tip #80: Understand the learning curve. The more times you or your organization does anything the lower the cost becomes to do it.

Tip #81: A plan's schedule should keep your development groups moving at a steady jog with enough milestones that they know when to periodically sprint in order to get back on pace. If a plan depends on the team's sprinting the entire length of a project, they won't make it. Similarly, the team won't make it if the team doesn't know when they need to sprint (and they always will need to sprint).

Tip #82: There are only four ways to measure results:

1) Quality: compare with history/market, engineering, or expectations.
2) Quantity: $, % ratio, degree, $/unit number, positive, or zero.
3) Timeliness: delivery, history, market, engineering expectations.
4) Cost: $, $/unit, ratio, positive, negative or zero.

Tip #83: Capital serves as a "safety net," allowing higher risk/higher gain investments. The risk of a circus high-wire performer is falling. With a net, artists can perform higher-risk feats without the fear of dying. The main risk of a prudent investment lies in the timing of the return. If you have "spare" capital equal to only 2 months of costs and your investment's return unexpectedly takes 3 months to start, you will run out of cash and die. More capital gives your company a bigger net and allows greater risk but learn the difference between courage and stupidity.

Tip #84: Life is still unfair. Often you can't make the "best" decision without creating a new and potentially inferior decision because of time spent on analysis. Often the best decision comes from flipping a coin or doing both.

Tip #85: One way to dramatically increase output is to add 2 hours of project time a day. This adds 10 hours a week, which is a 50% increase in project time (30 hours vs. the normal 20). Add another 5 hours on Saturday and you've increased your output a net 75%. *But* make sure you are adding project time, not merely shifting work you normally would have tackled during the day but don't since you know you'll be working late.

Tip #86: Any business larger than a true one-person company requires team effort to succeed. There isn't an envelope back large enough to manage the entire company from, without delegation. What do you do when your dreams grow too large to execute by yourself? What happens when 7-day weeks and 20-hour days aren't long enough? You *must* learn to work through a team.

Tip #87: The future will happen whether your company is ready or not. But remember, the future leaves muddy footprints in the present.

"Forecasting is difficult, especially about the future."
- Victor Borge

Tip #88: *Focus, Focus, Focus*. Unwillingness to focus is the great failing of most companies. You can't go to college and major in everything! With rare exceptions, great athletes excel in one position in one sport. In a competitive environment, there aren't enough resources to invest in a successful run for the gold unless you focus on a *small* number of goals.

Tip #89: Everyone in the company is responsible for success. Failure is the exclusive fault of senior management.

Tip #90: People are a lot like the weather. The most accurate way to predict the weather is to assume it will be the same as yesterday. People are most likely to handle a problem the way they handled it in the past. When interviewing for a new position, always press candidates to discuss *specific* examples of how they handled things in previous jobs. A candidate's exhibited behaviors are more significant than experience.

Tip #91: Company culture starts at the top! Look around, ask yourself what *you* are doing to create and propagate the atmosphere and value system around you.

Tip #92: Remember the sea squirt. It uses its simple brain to locate a safe rock to attach to and then it eats its brain. We do not want sea squirts as employees.

Tip #93: No, Virginia, it isn't good enough for someone to *try*. Save us from executives who "try their best" to reach sales numbers, get a product out the door, or produce and deliver quality products on time. Listen to how a project will be done or why a job can't be done, but don't listen to "I'll try."

Tip #94: Don't be surprised that you have to "sell" benefits. It is human nature for people to be short-sighted and suspicious. Don't consider offering a new company benefit unless you stand ready to explain and sell it. Worse yet, there will *always* be someone who thinks it isn't enough and asks you to change or expand the benefit...sigh.

Tip #95: Don't have a goodbye celebration when an employee quits the company. Instead, always celebrate when another perceptive individual *joins.*

Tip #96: When an employee says they're underpaid, imagine they just quit and that you have to replace them. Ask a couple of recruiters what you would have to pay for a replacement. If the employee is underpaid, adjust their salary; if not, explain to them what you did and why their current salary reflects their fair market value.

Tip #97: Another communication technique: Have a gourmet bagel breakfast in front of your office once a week one hour before starting time. Rules: Everyone stands and eats the bagels there, and when the bagels are gone the function is over. This is just one of many ways to keep communication open. A lunchroom is a good investment for the same purpose. It fosters informal communication between departments. If you have enough employees, see if a local restaurant will set up a small food-service counter so folks from different departments can mingle over lunch without leaving the company.

Tip #98: In many companies, the only time you have a meeting is when you have bad news to report. Try this. Once a month, have a feel-good company luncheon. This informal event is hosted by one department and features simple fare like pizza. After lunch, recognize all employees who have a birthday that month (as a company grows, random birthday parties can be a significant drag on productivity), have new people introduce themselves, and announce and celebrate the month's accomplishments. The rule of this meeting is "good news only."

Tip #99: What do you do when an employee had an outstanding year, but an extra-high raise would upset the salary range for that position? Give that employee a one-time bonus along with a normal salary increase. This gives high achievers cash and recognition yet maintains the integrity of your company's salary structure.

Tip #100: Sales forecasts should be done to a consistent level of confidence. A sales forecast is actually a curve of probable values. Sales executives should provide a number with a sufficient confidence factor to support the operating budget, each number having an equal likelihood of being greater or less than the forecast. A typical confidence factor is 80% assuming that you can delay or accelerate expenditures in response to the actual results while sustaining existing investments.

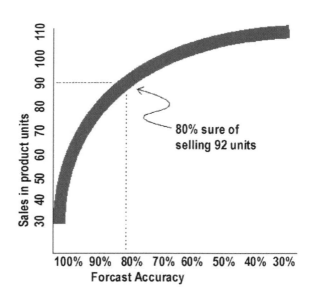

About the Author

John W. Myrna is cofounder of Myrna Associates Inc., a company that helps organizations thrive by facilitating new strategic plans, formulating actionable tactics, and evaluating workforce performance against those plans. For 30 years, his team has been helping clients create and grow value by turning their vision into reality using proprietary methodologies as part of intense, two-day off-site sessions. Along with a passion for teaching and his broad business experience and knowledge, John has a gift for bringing out the best in companies and their management teams.

In addition to regularly publishing articles and speaking to business audiences, John has contributed chapters on strategic business planning and implementation to The Business Expert Guide to Small Business Success and is the author of four previous books. He also coaches CEOs one-on-one.

Contact John via email at success@myrna.com, connect with johnwmyrna on LinkedIn, or visit his website at www.myrna.com.

Made in the USA
Columbia, SC
15 September 2023

22934740R00030